màu đỏ Mê Kông:

when the Mekong ran red

màu đỏ Mê Kông:

when the Mekong ran red

Tito Titus

For
Col, Liem, Miles, and Khai

Cargo

Vung Tau

1.

Helicopters: gnats massing
          around the Asian sun
       in the sky
       in my head
                   my brain

high yellow walls surround
the Buddhist temple
          polished white tiles
          at its golden gate say
                   hey—army boots—
          do not enter, người nước ngoài!

beside the ancient ornate gate—
a beggar sits cross-legged
pretends to be blind
          but turns away from my camera

across the street—
emaciated painted and sad
          women of pleasure
in diaphanous pyjamas
          slip into shadows

above—
olive drab helicopters
choppers, copters, thopters
          whirring humming thrumming
       drumming, strumming, coming

          and going
          all day

                   every day

       helicopters
       always
       always

                   always
 helicopters
 bombinate my brain.

2.

Vung Tau Officers Club
high concrete ceilings echo
Aretha Franklin—R-E-S-P-E-C-T
          alcohol pours
          brown amber and clear

Captains argue—
          Italy voted thirty percent communist!
          Will we go to war with Italy
          if they get fifty-one percent?
The domino theory says Asians will fall
          clackety-clack
          until Mao owns them all
                    clack-clack.

Table servers take home scraps
steak gristle and lettuce
to feed their families.
          Some here call them 'slopes'
          or 'gooks'
                    after they've gone.

Loud men's voices
slap white tile walls
          more alcohol
               more alcohol
               more alcohol
               thrum-a-dum-dum
               more alcohol

only curfew shuts their gullets.

3.

Quick-tongued house geckos
          catch crickets in the corners
          get fat off mosquitos, con muỗi

They crawl the walls and
          ceaselessly watch
          drunken men wearing saurian green.

A chunky man in combat boots
—the corps of engineers captain—
stands on a table
          grabs three inches of rough reptile
          swallows it whole
                    washes it down with Foster's

and the room erupts—
          military lizard men
          howl whoop and bay.

Oh shit
I'm in an inmate
in the asylum
          named war.

4.

A pagoda-shaped kiosk
serves French onion soup
and salade Niçoise
on the beach.

South China Sea waves
swaddle the sand
again and again.

The French
were shooed away in '54;
        the sea is warm
        as it was then.

The soup, its good;
tastes romantically Gallic
        between air raids.

Dong Tam

5.

An island of mud
dug from the swamp!

In monsoon season
diesel-powered pumps run daily.
They retrieve the saturated army base
            that endlessly spits itself
            back into the surrounding mire.

In any season
especially at night
storms of mortar shells
blast holes in rooftops
            like thunder fucks tin—

good reason for bunker town—
            a suburban subdivision of
            sandbag huts roofed by sheets of steel
                well-stocked with liquor
                poker chips and stories.

Don't go outside tonight
there are monsters
screaming monsters
dropping from the sky
                and they know
                where you are.

6.

Whistle boom
          I stumble in mud
whistle boom
          it's black-out time
whistle boom
          no lights allowed
whistle boom
          lost my glasses
whistle boom
          can't see
whistle boom
          on my hands and knees
whistle boom
          in monsoon muck
whistle boom
          where's my bunker?
whistle boom
          where am I?
whistle boom
          here's mud in your eye
                    w
                      h
                        i
                          s
                            t
                              l
                                e

                         boom.

Can Tho

IV CAN THO ARMY AIRFIELD

7.

Motorcycles, scooters, old black Citroëns,
cyclos: rickshaws on two-stroke petrol
rush through vendor-lined streets
horizontal waterfalls of wheels.

Watermelons and bananas
French bread and
fish pulled from the Mekong River
only blocks away.

Áo dài wearing women
black pantaloons and tunics
yellow, white, and red
beautifully flowing—
laughing apparitions.

See that palm tree?
The one with no top?
Mortar shell clipped it off.

Welcome to Can Tho—
bullseye of the Delta!
Your room will be on the roof
      where things that fall from the sky
               land first.

This, my new home
omphalos
the land inside the land
      that doesn't want me

pretending to be a man
          unafraid.

8.

A little French hotel
a lovely billet
in a city alive with busyness
Vietnamese guards sleep
        in a sandbagged hut in front
American soldiers inside
crawl beneath their beds
when the mortar storm
blows holes through
        the roof
            paper thin metal.

When the mortar storm blows over
someone pops a top
on a can of beer
tells a joke about Ho Chi Minh.

9.

On Christmas eve
the first sergeant
a tall black man
enters the cantina
dressed like Santa
says
    ho ho ho!

    LOUD!

The Vietnamese barmaid
screams
disappears

forever.

10.

On the airfield
twenty soldiers and twenty locals
warehouse for war
ship supplies across the Delta
        agricultural advisors
                or so we were told
        special forces and the CIA
        Navy river patrols—
                swift boats
        military advisors
        all the strays
exiles from chains of command.

Pushing paper pushing food
packing pallets stuffing planes
        high-winged bush planes
                called Beavers and Otters

        up and down all day

stuff comes in
stuff goes out
                steaks and lobster for the Navy
                bullets and beans for the Green Berets

helicopters whop and thwop
they never stop—
                Hueys, Chinooks, Cobras
                deafening turbines and rotor blades
                        ever on the move

Jeeps
and heavy trucks on a tear,
deuce-and-a-halfs with canvas canopies
        loading and unloading

rifles always ready

11.

A typical tropical day—
truck-sized coolers
          three thousand cubic feet each
we call them reefers
          white and chrome
          their buzzing motors drone.

Young men's bodies—
crammed, stacked, and wrapped
          in shiny black plastic bags—
          tagged and tied.

Steaming heat!
Close the door!
          Latch it tight
          keep the stink
                    inside.

This is the aftermath
of the '68 Tet Offensive.

12.

Rainy day
        muddy road
        sluggish puddles—

Jeep on a rip

See those áo dais? he says

Please no, I think

black water spatters over
        silk and rayon
        black, pink, red, and yellow

Wheeeeeeeee! he says

Shit, I think

Không có, they shriek.

Saigon / Tan Son Nhut

13.

Cobra helicopter
built to kill
shaped like a flying shark
          rotors and rockets
          multi-barrel rotary machine guns
          grenade launchers
          and cannons
sits beside my bed
all day every day
all night every night
the snake from the sky
at my window

sun crusted blood
baking on broken
Cobra canopy glass
          and thick soupy
          merlot in the cockpit
where the pilot sat
until the day
The Snake rested
by my pillow.

14.

Holiday rivers
firecracker paper
          ankle deep red
flowing through streets
          like blood running
over graves.

15.

United States military officers
gentlemen, they say
hail a cyclo-cab
        two-cycle engine cackling
        pulling a pedicab without the pedi.

The driver, a young and tired man,
meets America's finest, two of them.
They speak of piastres and dollars and back again
        quibble about numbers on paper—
        international diplomacy.

The finance captain, two silver bars on his shoulder,
            the third of these olive-uniformed warriors,
pulls out his pecker and pisses
on the cyclo passenger seat,
raises his arms high, waves at the sky,
loudly declares—

        Win their hearts and minds!

16.

SHORT!

We shout it every day
when days remaining
        can be counted
        on hands and feet

Hey fat boy
        you short?
Hell yeah
        I'm short—
short as your girlfriend's pussy hair,
        I'm short.

But Lenny from Arkansas?
Standing in line on the tarmac
waiting to board
        the Pan American freedom bird
            first stop—Hawaii,
a wild ass mortar shell
picks him out, takes him down.

He's Lenny-in-a-box now
will change planes
        in Oakland.

It isn't easy
        being short.

17.

So long

  Vinh Long
  Dong Tam
  Vung Tau
  Bac Lieu
  Binh Tre
  My Tho
  Chau Doc
  Long Xuyen
  Soc Trang
  Ca Mau
  Tra Vinh
  Saigon
  Mekong
  Vietnam.

I'm gone.

1968 in three easy pieces

I remember it differently every time.

Sometimes—
       I drop from the sky like an American boulder
       on the Cambodian border.

       The plane, coyly called a Beaver, hits the ground
       wheels-and-nose first,
          flips tail-forward, stops cold,
          upside down.

       I survive the crash, but die
       and rise—how I rise!—to the sky,
       AK-47 fire glowing in my ass,
       my legs awkwardly twisted.

Most times—
       We descend like a re-entry rocket
       and smell like blue smoke.
       Oil flows like a river
          across our single-engine cowling,
          that blinds the cockpit window.

       Now here's the part I want you to believe:
          I didn't stare at the floor
          didn't pray like a newborn convert,
          didn't beg for more calendar
          didn't break a whitened finger
             with a fast grab at something
             anything to hold onto.

       Oh, no. Not that.

I waved to the disappearing sky,
like a rodeo cowboy,
leaned back, cried out,
What a helluva ride!
We're going home, folks!

Of course I did. Sure.

But sometimes—

I pull a poem from an airplane belly,
    imagine it's my last ride
    and say to the pilot—

Is this a good time?

 មេគង្គ ក្រហម

Cambodia, 1995

Tuol Sleng in the Summertime

Khmer Rouge leader Pol Pot converted Tuol Sleng, once a Phnom Penh high school, into a torture and execution center. It operated from 1975 to 1979 during the Khmer Rouge's horrific reign over Cambodia. Scattered Khmer Rouge contingents continued to fight as a guerrilla force until 1998 when Pol Pot died during house arrest by a renegade rebel faction. I visited Tuol Sleng in 1995.

As a teenager, my friend Hoa escaped the genocidal madness of late-seventies Cambodia. He walked four-hundred-sixty miles—hiding, dodging, evading—through assassin-controlled farmlands, villages, and jungles, to reach safety in Thailand. Sixteen years later, as the owner of a luncheonette noodle shop in Seattle, he received news about his aged and ailing father. He wanted to return home to Kampong Cham and invited me to come along. We flew to Phnom Penh via Seoul and Singapore.

By the time Vietnam drove the Khmer Rouge out of Phnom Penh, Pol Pot's regime had killed up to two million people—roughly twenty percent of Cambodia's population—by forced labor, starvation, torture, and execution. Most of those who died were ethnic minorities (including several in Hoa's own Chinese family), intellectuals, and businesspeople. By the end, they were murdering people who wore glasses—suspected readers and therefore presumed highbrows. Testing the limits of euphemism, historians call it *a program of radical social and agricultural reform.*

During our visit, Khmer Rouge units still controlled some rural and forested areas, particularly in the northern and western regions. The day Hoa and I purchased our charter plane tickets in a dimly-lit

Cambodian restaurant in south Seattle, I spied an outdoor magazine cover on a drugstore rack. It said something like this: *Visit Beautiful Cambodia, See Amazing Things, and Maybe Die.* But it was the chance of a lifetime, and I wasn't turning back. I felt as if I'd surrendered my will to kismet.

Singapore's SilkAir landed us at Phnom Penh International Airport. Ten customs and visa checkers, each armed with a variety of colorful rubber stamps and stickers, sat behind a long line of little desks. They all appeared zealously important and official, and each expected monetary gratitude.

Hoa's uncle, a jeweler, miraculously survived the pogroms. After securing lodging at his home, we reported to the American Consulate. The officer advised us not to ride trains, not to go out at night, and to stay the hell out of areas known to be controlled by the Khmer Rouge. (The beautiful beaches of Battambang would have to wait for another time.) The trains were often ambushed cowboy movie style—sometimes by the Khmer Rouge, sometimes by the military. The Khmer Rouge bushwhackers sought Europeans and Americans for their ransom value. The soldiers who attacked the trains looked for quick cash and food. They hadn't been paid in months.

We traveled by rented car, a rattling dented sunburned Datsun, from Phnom Penh to Hoa's hometown—Kampong Cham. At certain intervals, his family asked me to sit on the floor in the back seat area so that I wouldn't be seen by potentially dangerous characters. They were remarkably protective throughout my stay.

All the way, we listened to Cambodian rock music. Once, bumping along on the rugged road, I said, Wow! That's Cambodian rap!

Someone corrected me, *No. That's Khmer rap.*

My Chinese hosts were national Cambodians, but they were not a part of the dominant Khmer culture or governance. They wanted me to understand that, especially considering recent history.

We whizzed past sixteen-foot-tall ant hills, cheerful children herding spindle-shanked cattle, stilt houses, scattered palms, and seemingly endless miles of flat fields with almost-orange soil.

In the fresh shadow of Cambodia's recent history of butchery, Hoa's family didn't understand why we wanted to visit the Tuol Sleng Genocide Museum in Phnom Penh. Twelve to fourteen thousand died from torture and execution there, depending on who's estimating. Hoa's sister—who insisted on carrying my things while walking ten feet behind me whenever we went shopping—asked me through his translation, *Why do you want to go there?*

Because I want to see what it was like, I said.

It was horrible! Everyone knows that! I still don't know why you go!

With family listening, perhaps eight people of all ages gathered around, my words translated by Hoa and his adorable chubby aunt, I talked about the World War II Holocaust. I told them that, just as in Cambodia, many people were targeted, but that Jewish people bore the brunt of the mass killings.

A twenty-something male cousin interjected. *My Grandfather,* he said in English, then made the sound and lateral finger motion of his throat being slit.

I continued—Jews observe Yom HaShoah, a day to remember the genocide committed upon their people. In the West, it's called Holocaust Remembrance Day, or

Holocaust Day. There are museums and memorials in many places. They want to remember what happened because they don't want to let it happen again.

Ahhhhh, said Hoa's sister. Around us, her family nodded solemnly. I'm not sure, though, whether she understood or simply wanted to end the discussion. Perhaps both.

We went the next day.

Most of Hoa's extended family waited outside while he, one of his brothers, and I toured the premises with an English-speaking guide. We saw the racks and shackles hanging from former classroom walls; and nearby, rust-spackled military cot frames with wrist and ankle restraints at each corner. Our guide described torture methods—extracting fingernails, pouring alcohol on wounds, forcing prisoners' heads under water.

The dimly lit rooms smelled tropically fusty and stale. Their walls displayed thousands of faded black-and-white headshots annotated with prisoner numbers. I wondered how many of them attended Tuol Sleng when it served as a high school. And I pondered the similarity of communist Khmer Rouge record keeping and WWII German Nazi archiving. What is it about genocidal annihilation that makes the perpetrators keep such exacting records of the dead? Even serial murderers do it. They remember where they put the bodies. Is it similar to collecting pornography, as if one more named and numbered sepia headshot will never be enough to sustain gratification?

Tuol Sleng (or S-21, as the Khmer Rouge called it) wasn't a true prison. Rather, it served as a torture and execution center, a transition facility located between arrest and death a couple of days later. A

September 2011 *Financial Times* article described the operation this way:

Only fourteen people survived Tuol Sleng. One was Vann Nath, an artist, a good one. He outlasted the horror factory by painting and sculpting facsimiles of Khmer Rouge leader Pol Pot, something enjoyed and demanded by Kaing Guek Eav, S-21's commander—known as Comrade Duch. Nath's post-Khmer Rouge paintings and drawings, displayed in the last S-21 room we visited, documented the atrocities that occurred there— a hog-tied prisoner's throat slashed by a military-appearing man, a child stabbed with a bayonet, a man's fingernails ripped away by guards, and suchlike.

We saw an array of Nath's work. His paintings and drawings portrayed elongated limbs and emaciated faces of the victims. In some of them, his style during those years reminded me of paintings and sketches by Egon Schiele, the Austrian Expressionist painter and protégé of Gustav Klimt. Critics often found Schiele's work as being grotesque, erotic, pornographic, or otherwise disturbing.

Schiele and his wife died within three days of each other, both by Spanish Flu, in 1918. Fifteen years later, when Adolf Hitler seized power, he ordered Nazi authorities to seize any art that didn't merit his Führer-istic aesthetic approval. That of course included Egon Schiele's work, what they could find of it. As World War II commenced, secret Schiele stashes spread across eastern Europe. That courageous Czechoslovakian resistance to military occupation allowed my fortunate visit to Schiele's principal museum in Český Krumlov, Czech Republic, fifty years later.

There's some historical resonance here, some circularity. Surely Hitler wouldn't have approved of Nath's post-killing-fields art any more than Schiele's angularly distorted figures, also with haunting eyes. But walls covered with black-and-white mug shots, those most likely could've stayed—so similar, as they were, to Third Reich ways of doing business.

An innocent who never knew why the Khmer Rouge arrested him, Vann Nath later toured the world, spoke to audiences and accepted recognition from art schools in Europe and United States. He held, for a time, residency at Rhode Island's Providence College. He also testified at Comrade Duch's trial.

During the late 1990s, Nath redirected his work from the macabre to childhood memories, pastoral landscapes, and traditional festivals. We can only imagine the internal torment, the survivor's guilt, he must have endured. Historian David Chandler said of Nath, *He was a lighthouse of regret and concern about this whole period.* He died in Phnom Penh at sixty-six.

Comrade Duch received a thirty-five-year sentence. He appealed. So did the prosecutors. In 2011 the Extraordinary Chambers in the Courts of Cambodia sentenced him to life imprisonment, the maximum allowed. He died at Khmer Soviet Friendship Hospital in Phnom Penh in September 2020. He was seventy-seven. The Khmer Rouge's most efficient executioner saw ten more years than Vann Nath. If life isn't fair, here's a case in point.

Then again, perhaps pain from Comrade Duch's *regret and concern about the whole period* exceeded Nath's. If so, he had to deal with ten more years of it.

Sometimes we jokingly say that something can't be unseen. For me, that's Tuol Sleng. But it's not a joke.

A week after our visit to Tuol Sleng, Hoa and I flew in a twin piston-engine plane from Phnom Penh to Siem Reap via Royal Air Cambodge, the airline with loose bolts bouncing on the wings. We stayed at a modest wood-frame guest house. Now, Siem Reap features over two-hundred luxury hotels. During our stay, there were none. Nearby Angkor Wat provides the big draw—the world's largest assemblage of religious structures and one of its most dramatic ancient ruins.

With even more of Hoa's extended family, we spent two days investigating lotus bud-shaped towers, cruciform terraces, narrative bas-relief scenes on walls, passageways, and galleries. Many of the centuries-old sculptures, both Hindu and Buddhist, were destroyed by the Khmer Rouge. I saw beautiful Buddha-head effigies, twelve-feet tall, knocked asunder, lying on the ground in pieces. But most remained, standing tall and stoically resolute—although severely eroded by seven hundred years of weather.

One evening back at our guest house, I met a young German couple in the hallway. We chatted. They too had visited Tuol Sleng, seen its horrors, walked through its gloom.

It's so tragic, the wife said to me in her clipped accent. *The whole world has to know what happened here!*

I kept the irony to myself.

អត្ថាធិប្បាយ

At least twelve genocidal campaigns—deliberate and systematic destruction of a racial, ethnic, political, or cultural group—already bloodstain the twenty-first century. Victims include Tamils in Sri Lanka, Muslims in Chechnya, pygmies in Democratic Republic of Congo, Tibetans and Uyghurs in China, Rohingyas and other ethnic minorities in Myanmar, Nuers (and possibly Dinkas) in South Sudan, Tigrayans in the western Amhara region of Ethiopia, Muhamasheen and Houthis in Yemen, Bosniaks (Muslims) in Bosnia, Palestinians in Gaza, and Ukrainians—at the hands of Russian military—in their own country.

In addition to wholesale killing, the 1948 United Nations Genocide Convention includes in its genocide definition . . . *forcible transferal of the* [targeted] *group children to another group.*[1] It's less bloody, but effectively advances the cultural-destruction aims of perpetrators. The practice raises less consternation or ire than does mass murder, but nonetheless advances the aggressors' genocidal aims. We've recently seen children victimized this way—abduction, forced relocation, cultural reeducation—in Ukraine, Tibet, and in China's Xinjiang province (Uyghurs).

---

[1] Article 2 of the 1948 accords defines genocide as any of the following acts committed with intent to destroy, in whole or in part, a national, ethnic, racial or religious group, as such: "killing members of the group; causing serious bodily or mental harm to members of the group; deliberately inflicting on the group conditions of life calculated to bring about its physical destruction in whole or in part; imposing measures intended to prevent births within the group; and, forcibly transferring children of the group to another group."

From various sides, politicians, academics, commentators, activists, propagandists, and diplomats argue endlessly about whether one thing or another constitutes genocide, whether the 1948 accords apply in one situation or another, whether the accords are "valid," as well as whether thus-and-such reported aggressions even happened. Denials, disagreements and alternative interpretations abound throughout all the barbarities listed above. Moreover, forty-one countries, mostly in Africa and Southeast Asia, refuse to join the 1948 Convention. These debates suggest that perhaps terms such as "atrocities" and "war crimes" are more useful and meaningful than "genocide."

Could genocide happen in the United States? Why not? I think it could. In 2018-19, by Executive Order, thousands of children were separated from their asylum-seeking immigrant parents, mostly at the Texas border, and were farmed out to various adoptive institutions. Some were eventually reconnected but, due to inconsistent and incomplete records, we don't know the exact number of children who remain separated. At the time, some of us argued that these official actions crossed the line established by the 1948 Convention's Article 2. These arguments were generally regarded as political hyperbole and were ignored by the government, media, and public.

Nonetheless, the 2018 turn in immigration policy, not to mention the mass relocation of Japanese-American citizens during World War II, illustrates how rapidly the unthinkable becomes thinkable, even doable. Despite millions of non-military Cambodian and Vietnamese deaths caused by American bombers, public opinion supporting the Vietnam War remained strong throughout its execution.

We ride a sharp and slippery fulcrum through history. Events and opinions can swing this way or that faster than you can say insurrection. History, with saddening side-steps and repetition, dances around our decades like an Appalachian snake-handler. Sometimes people get bitten.

Some historians and philosophers claim we live in the most peaceful era in human history.

Leaving Cambodia

Two years after the United Nations 1993 plebiscite
to stabilize the country, the Khmer Rouge still
occupied rural and uninhabited regions of
Cambodia and sometimes caused trouble in cities.
The Khmer Rouge particularly targeted the ethnic
Chinese minority, who included my hosts.

This clan, this *jiāzú*—
from dirt-kneed toddlers,
to elders, spindly from tropical aging—
this Chinese family, the Chuongs,
stays home tonight.

In nostalgic stillness,
midnight air hangs, blackened by hours,
dampened by yesterday's steamed air—
             Phnom Penh dew.

They speak warmly with light voices
             in night quiet.
Auntie Mei serves
unforgettably-mild green tea,
      again and again.

Hoa gives his brothers boxing gloves,
Souvenirs of America, he says,
and his sister, sitting on the floor,
nurses her baby and laughs.

Cousin Bai recalls uncles, aunts, a grandfather—
murdered in the fields,
tortured in Tuol Sleng.
      Bai's lips become thin, his voice tight
             like a taut rubber band.
      He slices his throat with his finger.

Auntie serves more tea.
Will this help my cold? I ask.
She laughs. She's a jubilant survivor.
I don't know! she says, and pours more tea.
Hoa raises his cup:
Next year, my brothers,
we meet again in beloved Phnom Penh.
But the Chuongs don't understand
      what he's doing or what he means.

Across the courtyard's dusty floor,
explosive light flashes the night,
illuminates our high terra cotta walls
topped with broken glass and barbed wire.
The dog awakens, bellows a startled bark;
earthen barricades echo his awakened voice.

Outside our residential ramparts—
minutes after the explosion—
soldiers shout and their Rottweilers
snoop about the dimly-lit street.

On a sunny afternoon in downtown Siem Reap

He stood before me barefoot,
his military greens torn and dirty,
on makeshift crutches, sticks really,
missing one leg—blown away by landmine.

He forced a sunshiny smile beneath
the shadow of matted black hair
falling over his forehead
and we made a deal.

I would take his photograph,
pay him four thousand riel—
roughly one American dollar—
and I still feel like a swindler.

Acknowledgements

Thank you, Hoa Chuong, wherever you are, for the adventure of a lifetime.

Thank you, Scott Ezell, for your expertise, wisdom, and assistance in preparing this chapbook for publication.

Thank you, Kate Titus, for supporting my trip to Cambodia when the country was still unsteady, and for the beautiful romantic comedy that we have created together.

Photo credits

Page 10, massing helicopters; Department of Defense, public domain.

Page 16, Dong Tam, monsoon mud, tents, and bunkers, 1968; The Delta Dragon, www.cantho-rvn.org/

Page 20, Can Tho Army Airfield, 1968; The Delta Dragon, www.cantho-rvn.org/

Page 28, wrecked Cobra warship helicopter ("The Snake"), Gemini AI rendering depicting the author's description of the dead and bloodied machine beside his bed where he slept at Tan Son Nhut Air Base during the Tet Offensive of 1968.

Page 34, Vietnamese guard standing outside platoon billet in downtown Can Tho, 1968; photograph by author.

Page 38, skulls stacked inside the Tuol Sleng Genocide Museum, Phnom Penh, 1995; photograph by author.

Page 55, one of several victim mugshot walls, as they existed in 1995, Tuol Sleng Genocide Museum; public domain.

Author

Tito Titus is the author of *I can still smile like Errol Flynn* (Empty Bowl Press, 2015). He appeared in 2020 on Garrison Keillor's "The Writer's Almanac". In 2023, he contributed to *I Sing the Salmon Home*, an anthology curated by former Washington State Poet Laureate Rena Priest. His satire appeared in *Puget Soundings*, *Argus*, and the *Seattle Post-Intelligencer*. During 1967-68, as a U.S. Army lieutenant, he served as a platoon leader in the 53rd Logistical Support Command, Mekong Delta, Vietnam.